Children's Songs for Harmonica.

ISBN: 978-0-7119-2831-2

Visit Hal Leonard Online at
www.halleonard.com

Contact us:
Hal Leonard
7777 West Bluemound Road
Milwaukee, WI 53213
Email: info@halleonard.com

In Europe, contact:
Hal Leonard Europe Limited
42 Wigmore Street
Marylebone, London, W1U 2RY
Email: info@halleonardeurope.com

In Australia, contact:
Hal Leonard Australia Pty. Ltd.
4 Lentara Court
Cheltenham, Victoria, 3192 Australia
Email: info@halleonard.com.au

How To Hold The Harmonica

Hold the harmonica in your left hand with the lowest note to the left.
Place your right hand in the position shown below.
The numbering system (1 - 16) used throughout the book represents the holes on the harmonica. Number one (1) the lowest note up to number sixteen (16) which is the last and highest note.

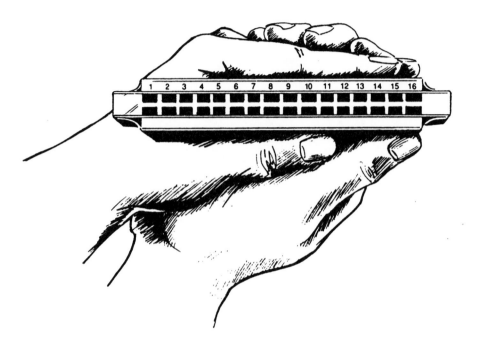

Breath Control

It is important for you to know how to breathe properly while playing. A lot of harmonica players use breath control to great effect as it enhances their playing. As you progress through this book you will find that your breath control ability will improve, at least for harmonica playing.

It is quite simple. All you have to do is inhale through your nose on a draw note (▼) and exhale through your nose on a blow note. (▲)

Notes On The Harmonica

↟ Upward arrows indicate: blow into your harmonica (blow notes)

↡ Downward arrows indicate: draw in your breath (draw notes)

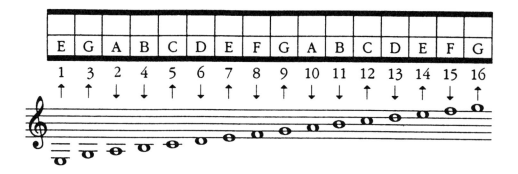

Play A Scale

The first thing we will learn to play on the harmonica is the C scale.
Try to play each note clearly without interference from neighbouring notes.
This may be tedious at first, however with a little practice you will soon be
able to play each individual note.

The 'C' Scale

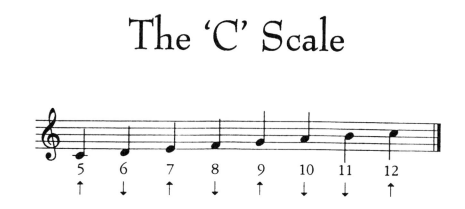

Silent Night

Peacefully

Si -	lent	night,		ho -	ly	night,
9	10	9	7	9	10	9	7
↑	↓	↑	↑	↑	↓	↑	↑

All	is	calm,	all	is	bright,
13	13	11	12	12	9
↓	↓	↓	↑	↑	↑

Round	yon	vir -	gin,	mo -	ther	and	child,
10	10	12	11	10	9	10	9	7
↓	↓	↑	↓	↓	↑	↓	↑	↑

Ho -	ly	in -	fant	so	ten -	der	and	mild,
10	10	12	11	10	9	10	9	7
↓	↓	↑	↓	↓	↑	↓	↑	↑

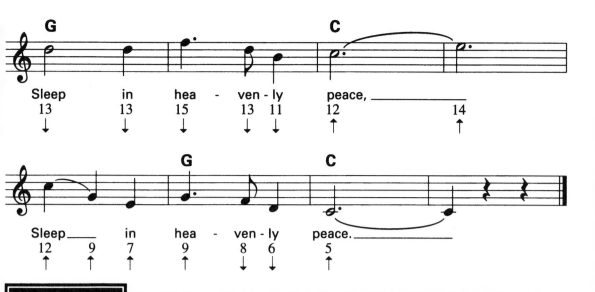

Sleep in hea - ven - ly peace, _____
13   13   15   13 11   12   14
↓   ↓   ↓   ↓   ↓   ↑   ↑

Sleep ____ in hea - ven - ly peace. _____
12   9   7   9   8   6   5
↑   ↑   ↑   ↑   ↓   ↓   ↑

ranges & Lemons

Moderately

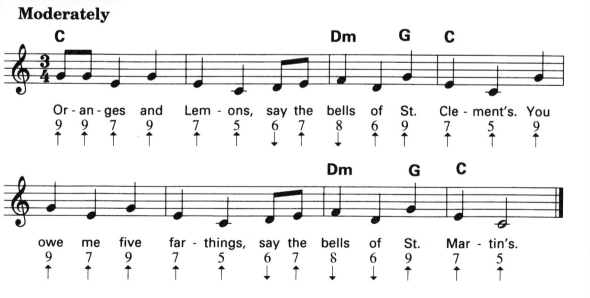

Or - an - ges and Lem - ons, say the bells of St. Cle - ment's. You
9   9   7   9   7   5   6   7   8   6   9   7   5   9
↑   ↑   ↑   ↑   ↑   ↑   ↓   ↑   ↓   ↑   ↑   ↑   ↑   ↑

owe me   five far - things, say the bells of St. Mar - tin's.
9   7   9   7   5   6   7   8   6   9   7   5
↑   ↑   ↑   ↑   ↑   ↓   ↑   ↓   ↓   ↑   ↑   ↑

Baa, Baa Black Sheep

Moderately

Baa,	baa,	black	sheep,	have	you	a -	ny	wool?
5↑	5↑	9↑	9↑	10↓	11↓	11↓	9↑	9↑

Yes,	sir,	yes,	sir,	three	bags	full;
8↓	8↓	7↑	7↑	6↓	6↓	5↑

One	for	the	mas -	ter,	and	one	for	the	dame,	and
9↑	9↑	9↑	8↓	8↓	8↓	7↑	7↑	7↑	6↓	6↓

one	for	the	lit -	tle	boy	that	lives	down	the	lane.
9↑	9↑	9↑	8↓	9↑	10↓	8↓	7↑	6↓	6↓	5↑

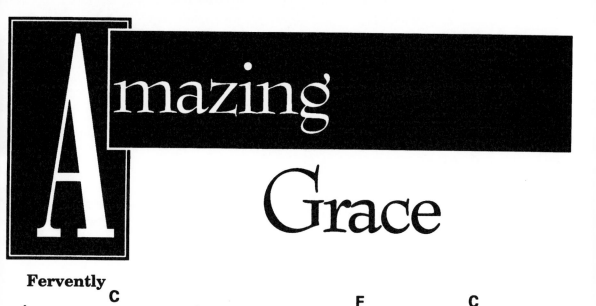

Amazing Grace

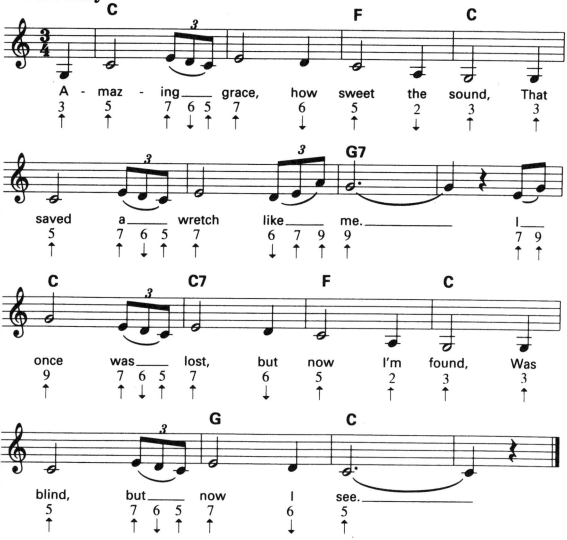

Fervently

C   F   C

A - maz - ing___ grace, how sweet the sound, That
3   5   7 6 5   7   6   5   2   3   3
↑   ↑   ↑ ↓ ↑   ↑   ↓   ↑   ↓   ↑   ↑

                    G7

saved a___ wretch like___ me.___ I___
5   7 6 5   7   6 7 9   9   7 9
↑   ↑ ↓ ↑   ↑   ↓ ↑ ↑   ↑   ↑ ↑

C   C7   F   C

once was___ lost, but now I'm found, Was
9   7 6 5   7   6   5   2   3   3
↑   ↑ ↓ ↑   ↑   ↓   ↑   ↑   ↑   ↑

            G   C

blind, but___ now I see.___
5   7 6 5   7   6   5
↑   ↑ ↓ ↑   ↑   ↓   ↑

9

When The Saints Go Marching In

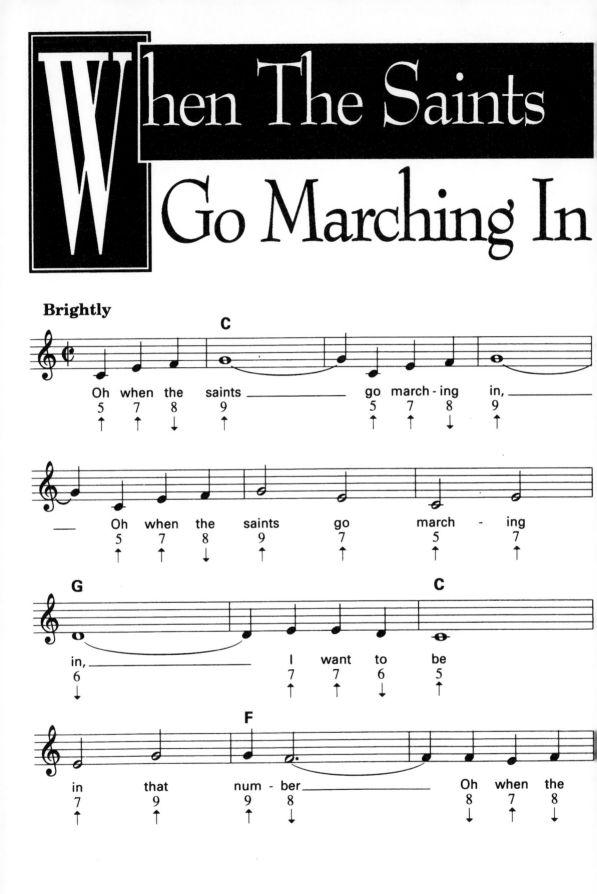

Brightly

Oh when the saints _____ go march-ing in, _____

_____ Oh when the saints go march - ing

in, _____ I want to be

in that num - ber _____ Oh when the

Jingle Bells

Brightly

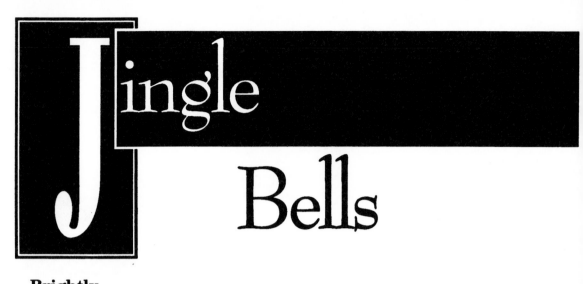

C

Jin - gle bells, jin - gle bells, jin - gle all the way,
7 7 7 7 7 7 7 9 5 6 7
↑ ↑ ↑ ↑ ↑ ↑ ↑ ↑ ↑ ↓ ↑

G7 C D

Oh what fun it is to ride in a one horse o - pen
8 8 8 8 8 7 7 7 7 7 6 6 7
↓ ↓ ↓ ↓ ↓ ↑ ↑ ↑ ↑ ↑ ↓ ↓ ↑

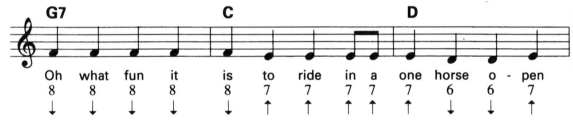

G C

sleigh, Oh jin - gle bells jin - gle bells,
6 9 7 7 7 7 7 7
↓ ↑ ↑ ↑ ↑ ↑ ↑ ↑

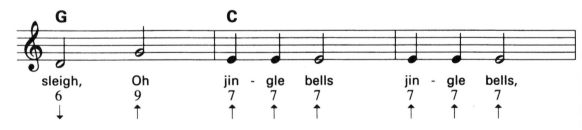

G7

jin - gle all the way, Oh what fun it
7 9 5 6 7 8 8 8 8
↑ ↑ ↑ ↓ ↑ ↓ ↓ ↓ ↓

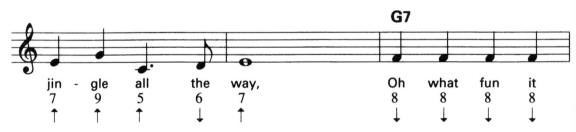

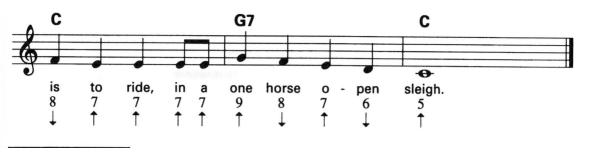

O Christmas Tree

Moderately

O Christ - mas tree, O Christ - mas tree, you stand in ver - dant
beau - ty O Christ - mas tree, O Christ - mas tree, you
stand in ver - dant beau - ty! Your boughs are green in
sum - mer's glow, And do not fade in win - ter's snow. O

Christ - mas tree, O Christ - mas tree, you stand in ver - dant beau - ty!
5 5 5 6 7 7 7 7 6 7 8 4 6 5
↑ ↑ ↑ ↓ ↑ ↑ ↑ ↑ ↓ ↑ ↑ ↓ ↓ ↑

This Old Man

Brightly

This old man, he played one, He played nick - nack
9   7   9   9   7   9   10 9   8   7
↑   ↑   ↑   ↑   ↑   ↑   ↓   ↑   ↓   ↑

on my thumb; With a nick - nack pad - dy whack,
6 7 8 7 8 9 5 5 5 5
↓ ↑ ↓ ↑ ↓ ↑ ↑ ↑ ↑ ↑

give a dog a bone, This old man came rol - ling home.
5 6 7 8 9 9 6 6 8 7 6 5
↑ ↓ ↑ ↓ ↑ ↑ ↓ ↓ ↓ ↑ ↓ ↑

15

Row, Row Your Boat

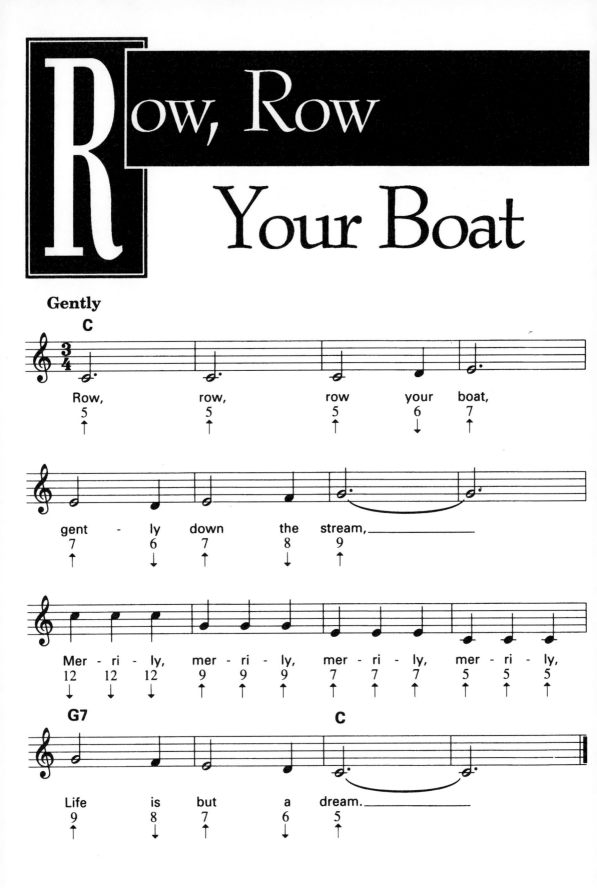

Polly Put The Kettle On

Cheerfully

Pol - ly	put	the	ket - tle	on,	Pol - ly	put	the	ket - tle	on,

Pol - ly put the ket - tle on,
9 ↑ 10 ↓ 9 ↑ 8 ↓ 7 ↑ 5 ↑ 5 ↑ 6 ↓ 7 ↑ 6 ↓ 5 ↑ 4 ↓ 3 ↑ 3 ↑

Pol - ly put the ket - tle on, we'll all have tea.
9 ↑ 10 ↓ 9 ↑ 8 ↓ 7 ↑ 5 ↑ 5 ↑ 7 ↑ 2 ↓ 4 ↓ 5 ↑

Su - key take it off a - gain, Su - key take it off a - gain,
7 ↑ 5 ↑ 8 ↓ 6 ↓ 7 ↑ 5 ↑ 5 ↑ 8 ↓ 2 ↓ 6 ↓ 5 ↑ 4 ↓ 3 ↑ 3 ↑

Su - key take it off a - gain they've all gone a - way.
7 ↑ 5 ↑ 8 ↓ 6 ↓ 7 ↑ 5 ↑ 5 ↑ 6 ↓ 2 ↓ 4 ↓ 4 ↓ 5 ↑

Twinkle, Twinkle Little Star

Quietly

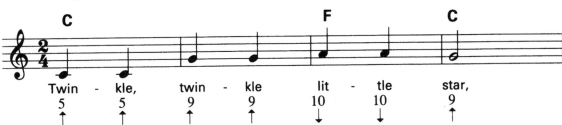

Twin - kle,	twin - kle	lit - tle	star,
5 5	9 9	10 10	9
↑ ↑	↑ ↑	↓ ↓	↑

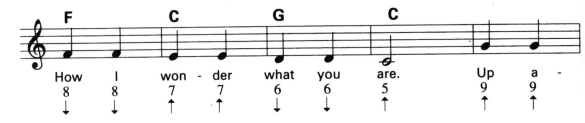

How	I	won - der	what	you	are.	Up	a -
8	8	7 7	6	6	5	9	9
↓	↓	↑ ↑	↓	↓	↑	↑	↑

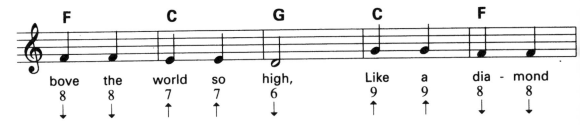

bove	the	world	so	high,	Like	a	dia - mond
8	8	7	7	6	9	9	8 8
↓	↓	↑	↑	↓	↑	↑	↓ ↓

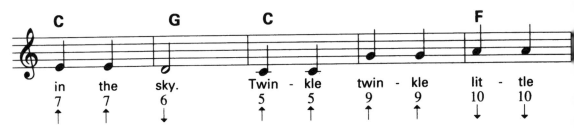

in	the	sky.	Twin - kle	twin - kle	lit - tle
7	7	6	5 5	9 9	10 10
↑	↑	↓	↑ ↑	↑ ↑	↓ ↓

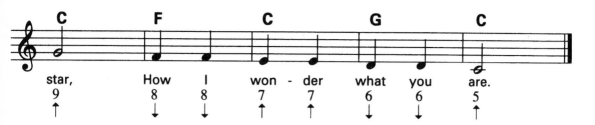

star,   How   I   won - der   what   you   are.
9   8   8   7   7   6   6   5
↑   ↓   ↓   ↑   ↑   ↓   ↓   ↑

Red River Valley

Moderately

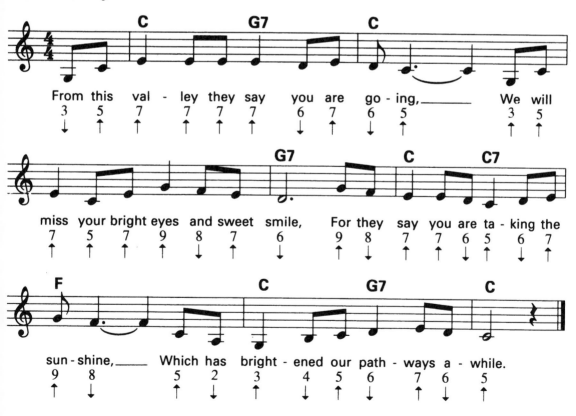

From this val - ley they say   you are   go - ing, _____   We will
3   5   7   7   7   7   6   7   6   5   3   5
↓   ↑   ↑   ↑   ↑   ↑   ↓   ↑   ↓   ↑   ↑   ↑

miss your bright eyes and sweet smile,   For they   say   you are ta - king the
7   5   7   9   8   7   6   9   8   7   7   6   5   6   7
↑   ↑   ↑   ↑   ↓   ↑   ↓   ↑   ↓   ↑   ↑   ↓   ↑   ↓   ↑

sun - shine, _____ Which has   bright - ened our path - ways a - while.
9   8   5   2   3   4   5   6   7   6   5
↑   ↓   ↑   ↓   ↑   ↓   ↑   ↓   ↑   ↓   ↑

London Bridge
Is Falling Down

Moderately

Lon - don Bridge is fal - ling down, fal - ling down, fal - ling down,
9 10 9 8 7 8 9 6 7 8 7 8 9
↑ ↓ ↑ ↓ ↑ ↓ ↑ ↓ ↑ ↓ ↑ ↓ ↑

Lon - don Bridge is fal - ling down my fair la - dy.
9 10 9 8 7 8 9 6 9 7 5
↑ ↓ ↑ ↓ ↑ ↓ ↑ ↓ ↑ ↑ ↑

Go Tell
Aunt Rhody

Moderately

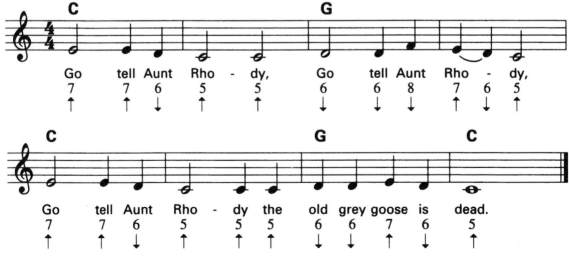

Go tell Aunt Rho - dy, Go tell Aunt Rho - dy,
7 7 6 5 5 6 6 8 7 6 5
↑ ↑ ↓ ↑ ↑ ↓ ↓ ↓ ↑ ↓ ↑

Go tell Aunt Rho - dy the old grey goose is dead.
7 7 6 5 5 5 6 6 7 6 5
↑ ↑ ↓ ↑ ↑ ↑ ↓ ↓ ↑ ↓ ↑

Home On The Range

Moderately

Oh, give me a home where the buf - fa - lo roam, Where the
deer and the an - te - lope play; Where
sel - dom is heard a dis - cour - ag - ing word, And the
skies are not clou - dy all day.

Jauntily

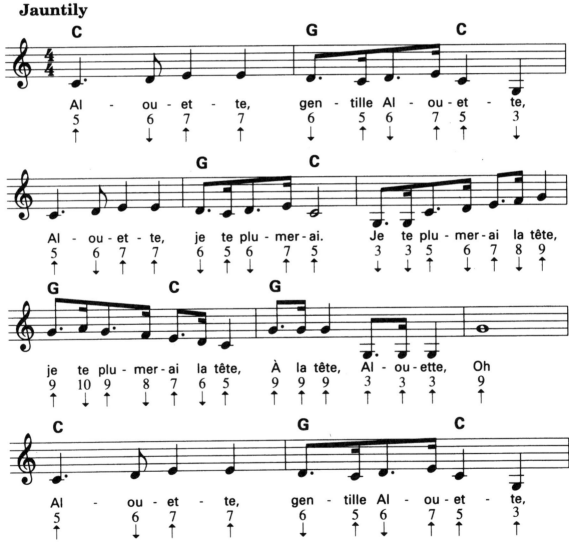

Al - ou - et - te, gen - tille Al - ou - et - te,

Al - ou - et - te, je te plu - mer - ai. Je te plu - mer - ai la tête,

je te plu - mer - ai la tête, À la tête, Al - ou - ette, Oh

Al - ou - et - te, gen - tille Al - ou - et - te,

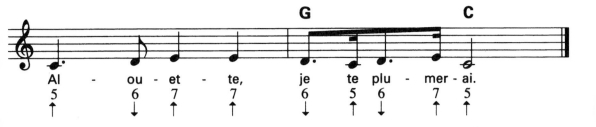

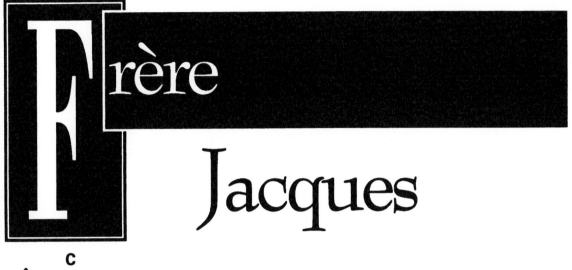

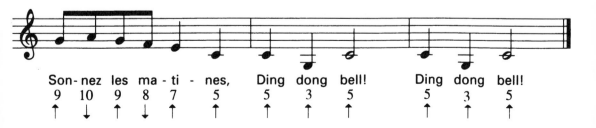

The Cradle Song

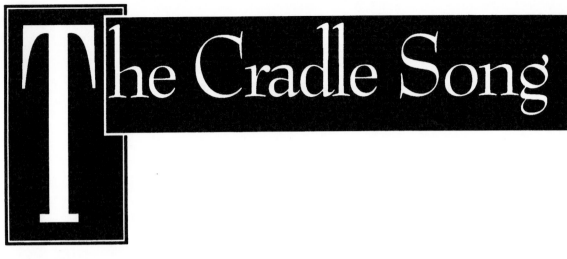

Slowly

Lull - a - by	and good -	night,	With	ros - es	de -
7 7 9	7 7	9	7 9	12 11	10

light. Creep in - to thy bed, There pil - low thy
10 9 6 7 8 6 6 7 8 6 8 11 10 9 11

head. If God will thou shalt wake, When the morn - ing doth
12 5 5 12 10 8 9 7 5 8 9 10

break, If God will thou shalt wake, When the morn - ing doth break.
9 5 5 12 10 8 9 7 5 8 7 6 5

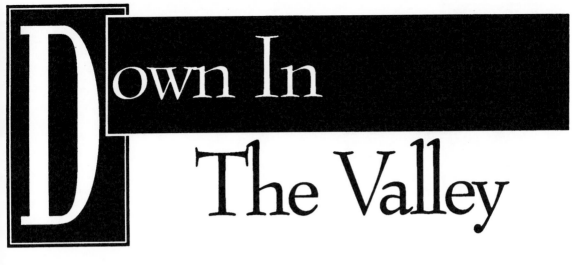

Down In The Valley

Flowingly

Down in the val - ley,_____ the
3 5 6 7 5 7

val - ley so low,_____
7 6 5 6

Hang your head o - ver,_____
3 4 6 8 6

hear the wind blow._____
4 5 6 5

25

Oh, Susanna

Lively

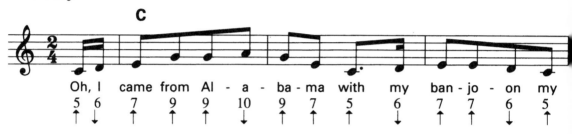

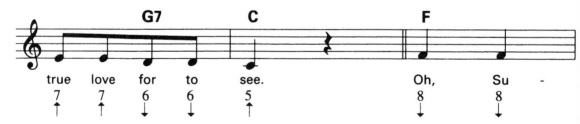

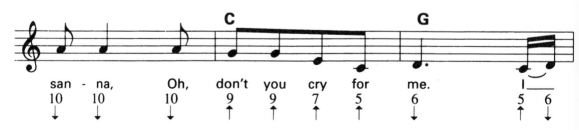

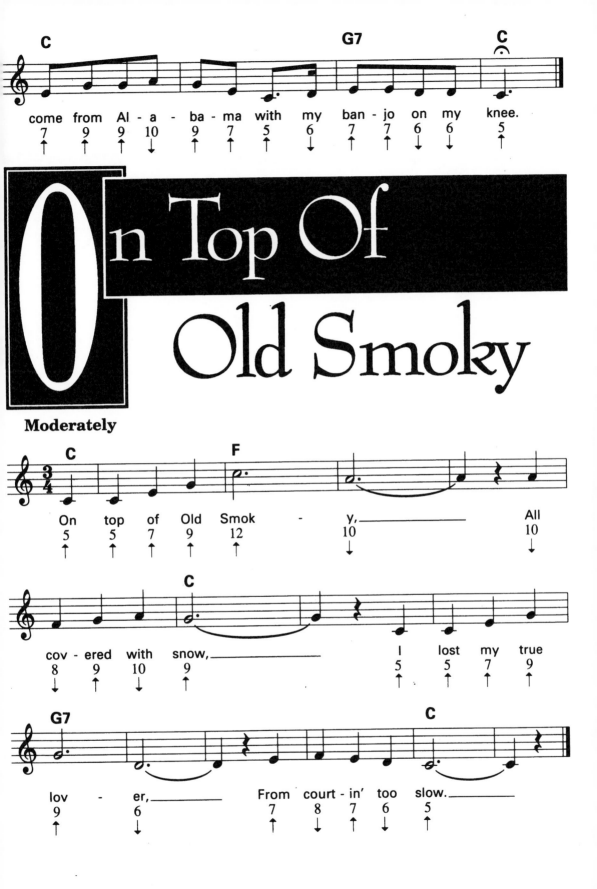

C   **G7**   **C**

come from Al - a - ba - ma with my ban - jo on my knee.
7   9   9   10   9   7   5   6   7   7   6   6   5

On Top Of Old Smoky

Moderately

C   **F**

On top of Old Smok - y, _____ All
5   5   7   9   12   10   10

C

cov - ered with snow,_____ I lost my true
8   9   10   9   5   5   7   9

G7   **C**

lov - er,_____ From court - in' too slow._____
9   6   7   8   7   6   5

27

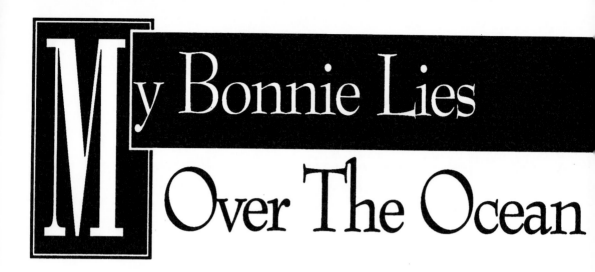

My Bonnie Lies Over The Ocean

With a lilt

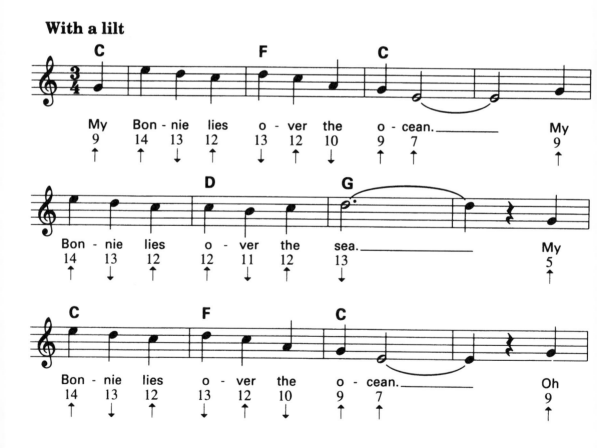

Buffalo Gals

Brightly

As I was ram - bling down the street,
5 7 7 8 8 10 9 7
↑ ↑ ↑ ↓ ↓ ↓ ↑ ↑

Down the street, Down the street, A beau - ty gal I
9 8 6 10 9 7 5 7 7 8 8
↑ ↓ ↓ ↓ ↑ ↑ ↑ ↑ ↑ ↓ ↓

chanc'd to meet, love - ly as morn - ing dew. Buf - fa - lo gals, can't you
10 9 7 12 11 9 8 6 5 5 5 5 7 10 10
↓ ↑ ↑ ↑ ↓ ↑ ↓ ↓ ↑ ↑ ↑ ↑ ↑ ↓ ↓

come out to - night? Come out to - night? Come out to - night?
10 9 9 7 9 8 8 6 10 9 9 7
↓ ↑ ↑ ↑ ↑ ↓ ↓ ↓ ↓ ↑ ↑ ↑

Buf-fa-lo gals can't you come out to-night, And dance by the light of the moon?
5 5 5 7 9 9 10 9 9 7 12 11 9 9 8 6 6 5

Skip To My Lou

Brightly

Fly's in the but-ter-milk, shoo fly shoo,
14 14 14 12 12 12 14 14 16

Fly's in the but-ter-milk,
13 13 13 11 11 11

shoo fly shoo,
13 13 15

Fly's in the but-ter-milk,
14 14 14 12 12 12

shoo fly shoo,
14 14 16

Skip to my Lou my dar - ling.
13 14 15 14 13 12 12

The Streets Of Laredo

Moderately

As I _____ walked out in the streets of La -
9   9   8   7   8   9   8   streets   6   5
↑   ↑   ↓   ↑   ↓   ↑   ↓   7↑   ↓   ↑

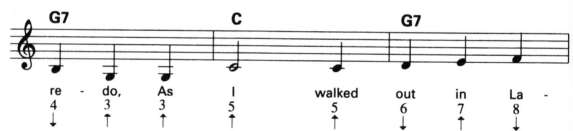

re - do, As I walked out in La -
4   3   3   5   5   6   7   8
↓   ↑   ↑   ↑   ↑   ↓   ↑   ↓

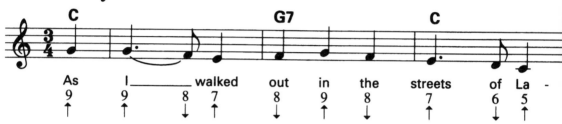

re - do one day, I spied a poor
7   6   5   6   9   9   8   7
↑   ↓   ↑   ↓   ↑   ↑   ↓   ↑

cow - boy all wrapped in white lin - en, All
8   9   8   7   6   5   4   3   3
↑   ↑   ↓   ↑   ↓   ↑   ↓   ↑   ↑

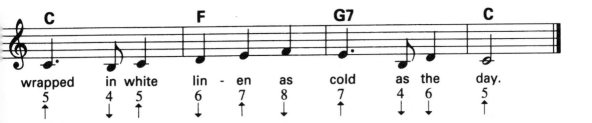

wrapped in white lin - en as cold as the day.
5 4 5 6 7 8 7 4 6 5
↑ ↓ ↑ ↓ ↑ ↓ ↑ ↓ ↓ ↑

Clementine

Moderately

In a cav - ern in a can - yon, Ex - ca -
12 12 12 10 14 14 14 12 12 14
↑ ↑ ↑ ↓ ↑ ↑ ↑ ↑ ↑ ↑

vat - ing for a mine Dwelt a min - er, for - ty
16 16 15 14 13 13 14 15 15 14 13
↑ ↑ ↓ ↑ ↓ ↓ ↑ ↓ ↓ ↑ ↓

nin - er, And his daugh - ter Clem - en - tine.
14 12 12 14 13 9 11 13 12
↑ ↑ ↑ ↑ ↓ ↑ ↓ ↓ ↑

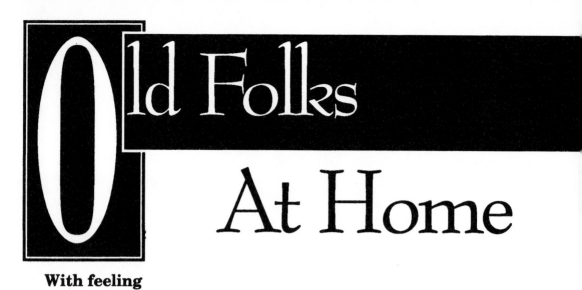

Old Folks At Home

With feeling

C	C7	F	C	G

Way down up-on the Swan-ee Riv-er, Far, far a-way,
7   6 5 7 6   5   12 10 12   9   7 5 6
↑   ↓ ↑ ↑ ↓   ↑   ↑   ↓ ↑   ↑   ↑ ↑ ↓

C	C7	F	C	G7	C

There's where my heart is turn-ing ev-er, There's where the old folks stay.
7   6 5 7 6   5   12 10 12   9   7 5 6 6   5
↑   ↓ ↑ ↑ ↓   ↑   ↑   ↓ ↑   ↑   ↑ ↑ ↓ ↓   ↑

G7	C	F	C	G7

All the world is sad and drear-y, Ev-'ry-where I roam,
11 12 13 9   9   10 9 12   12 10 8 10 9
↓   ↑   ↓   ↑   ↑   ↓   ↑ ↑   ↑   ↓   ↓ ↓   ↑

C	C7	F	C	G7	C

Oh, dar-lin's how my heart grows wea-ry, Far from the old folks at home.
7   6 5 7 6   5   12 10 12   9   7 5 6 7 6   5
↑   ↓ ↑ ↑ ↓   ↑   ↑   ↓ ↑   ↑   ↑ ↑ ↓ ↑ ↓   ↑

Yankee Doodle

The Yellow Rose Of Texas

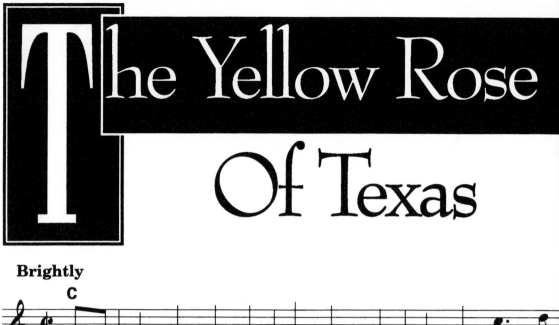

Brightly

meet	a - gain,	we	nev -	er -	more	will	part.
15 ↓	14 ↑	13 ↓	12 ↑	12 ↑	9 ↑	14 ↑	13 ↓ 12 ↑

Early One Morning

Brightly

Ear -	ly	one	mor –	ning	just	as	the	sun	was	ris -	ing	I
5 ↑	5 ↑	5 ↑	5 ↑	7 ↑	9 ↑	9 ↑	10 ↓	8 ↓	6 ↓	5 ↑	4 ↓	6 ↑ 3 ↓ 3 ↑

heard	a	poor	mai - den	in	the	val -	ley	be - low.	Oh	don't	de - ceive__	me,
5 ↑	5 ↑	5 ↑	5 ↑	7 ↑	9 ↑	9 ↑	10 ↓	8 ↓ 6 ↓ 4 ↓	5 ↑	6 ↓	7 ↑ 8 ↓ 9 ↑	7 ↑ 5 ↑

Oh	ne - ver	grieve__	me.	How__	could	I	leave__	a__	poor__	mai - den	so?
6 ↑	7 ↑	8 ↓	9 ↑	7 ↑ 5 ↑	5 ↑	7 ↑	9 ↑ 12 ↑	11 ↓	10 ↓ 9 ↑ 8 ↓	7 ↑ 6 ↓ 5 ↑	4 ↓ 5 ↑

Plaisir d'Amour

The Joys Of Love

Moderately

The joys of love
3 5 6 7

are but a mo - ment long,
7 8 8 7 5 7 6

The pain of lo - ve en -
3 2 4 5 6 7

dures the whole life long.
2 6 8 7 6 5

38

The Camptown Races

Energetically

The Camp-town la-dies sing this song, Doo-dah! doo-dah! The
Camp-town race-track five miles long, Oh, the _ doo-dah-day!

Chorus

Goin' to run all night, Goin' to run all day. I'll
bet my mon-ey on the bob-tail nag, Some-bod-y bet on the bay.

39

Swing Low Sweet Chariot

band__ of an-gels com-in' af-ter me,__ Com-in' for to car-ry me home.
10 9 7 7 5   5 5 5 5 2 3   5 5 5 5 7 7 6   5

Hush Little Baby

Quietly

Hush, lit-tle ba-by, don't say a word, Pa-pa's gon-na buy you a
3 7 7 7 8 7 6 6 6   3 3 6 6 6 6 7

mock - ing bird. And if the mock - ing
6 5 5 5 3 7 7 8

bird won't sing, Pa-pa's gon-na buy you a dia-mond ring.
7 6 6 3 3 6 6 6 6 7 6 5 5

41

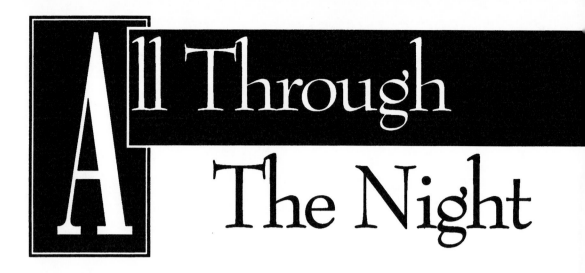

All Through The Night

Peacefully

Sleep, my child, and peace at-tend __ thee, All through the night; Guard - ian an - gels God will send __ thee, All through the night; Star of hope for ev - er peep - ing While the world is hushed and sleep - ing,

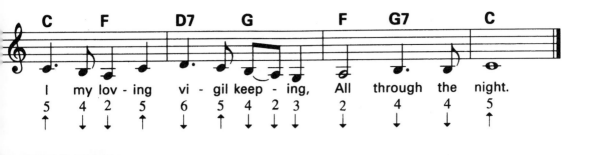

C	F	D7	G	F	G7	C

I my lov - ing vi - gil keep - ing, All through the night.

5 4 2 5 6 5 4 2 3 2 4 4 5
↑ ↓ ↓ ↑ ↓ ↑ ↓ ↓ ↓ ↓ ↓ ↓ ↑

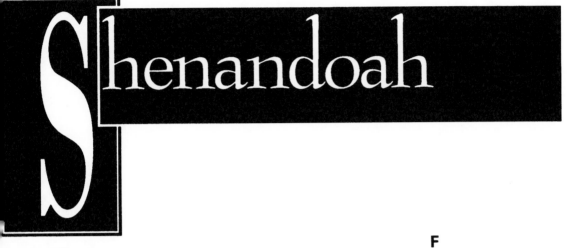

Shenandoah

C   **F**

mp

Oh, Shen - an - doah, ___ I long to hear you, ___ A - way, ___ you roll - ing

3 5 5 5 6 7 8 10 9 12 11 10 9 10 9
↑ ↑ ↑ ↑ ↓ ↑ ↓ ↓ ↑ ↑ ↓ ↓ ↓ ↓ ↑

C   **F**   **Am**

riv - er. Oh, Shen - an - doah, ___ I long to hear you, ___ A -

7 9 9 10 10 10 7 9 7 6 5 5 6
↑ ↑ ↑ ↓ ↓ ↓ ↑ ↑ ↑ ↓ ↑ ↑ ↓

C   **Em**   **G7**   **C**

way, ___ I'm bound - a - way, 'Cross the wide Mis - sou - ri.

7 5 4 7 9 5 6 7 6 6 5
↑ ↑ ↓ ↑ ↑ ↑ ↓ ↑ ↓ ↓ ↑

Dixie

With spirit

I wish I was in the land of cot-ton, Old times there are
not for-got-ten, Look a - way, look a - way, look a - way, Dix-ie-
land! In Dix - ie - land where I was born in Ear - ly on one

Home Sweet Home

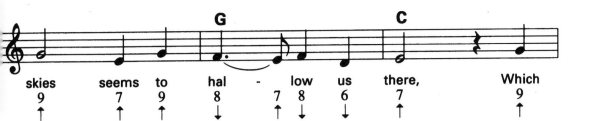

skies seems to hal - low us there, Which
9 7 9 8 7 8 6 7 9
↑ ↑ ↑ ↓ ↑ ↓ ↓ ↑ ↑

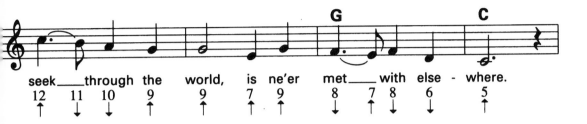

seek___through the world, is ne'er met___with else - where.
12 11 10 9 9 7 9 8 7 8 6 5
↑ ↓ ↓ ↑ ↑ ↑ ↑ ↓ ↑ ↓ ↓ ↑

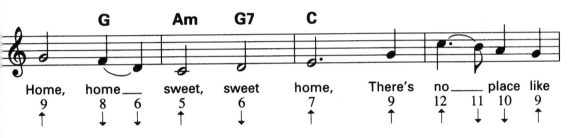

Home, home___ sweet, sweet home, There's no___ place like
9 8 6 5 6 7 9 12 11 10 9
↑ ↓ ↓ ↑ ↓ ↑ ↑ ↑ ↓ ↓ ↑

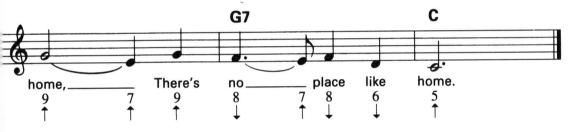

home,_____ There's no___ place like home.
9 7 9 8 7 8 6 5
↑ ↑ ↑ ↓ ↑ ↓ ↓ ↑

The Banks Of The Ohio

Tenderly

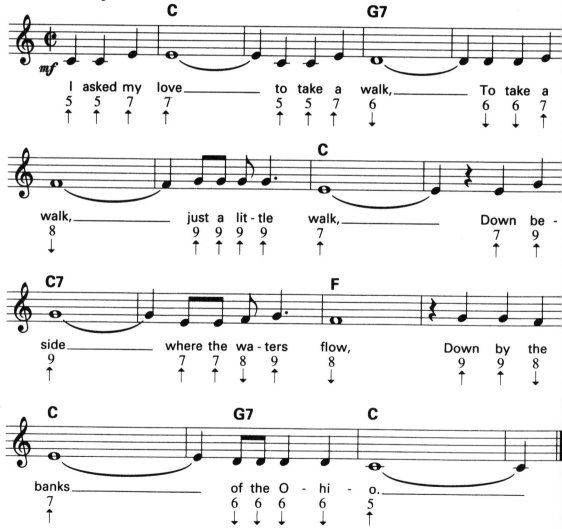

I asked my love to take a walk, To take a
walk, just a lit - tle walk, Down be -
side where the wa - ters flow, Down by the
banks of the O - hi - o.